FIRS HANDBOOK
ON
REFORMS
IN
THE TAX SYSTEM
(2004 - 2011)

FIRS HANDBOOK
ON
REFORMS
IN
THE TAX SYSTEM
(2004 - 2011)

A publication of the Federal Inland Revenue Service

FIRS
NIGERIA

Produced by
Safari Books Ltd
Ile Ori Detu
1, Shell Close, Onireke Ibadan
Email: safarinigeria@gmail.com

FIRS HANDBOOK ON REFORMS IN THE TAX SYSTEM
(2004 - 2011)

Published 2012

ISBN: 978-978-48776-8-8

Safari Books Ltd

Contents

Foreword   *iii*

Acknowledgements   *ix*

Chapter One
Brief History of Taxation in Nigeria   1
Chapter Two
Current Legislative Underpinning   5
Chapter Three
Reforms to date   9
Chapter Four
Revenue accruing to Governments for
Appropriation   45
Chapter Five
Recurring Issues and Challenges   51
Chapter Six
Global Tax Issues   61

Foreword

In 2003, the FIRS annual collection was 697.7 billion naira. This amount represented a deficit of 278.5 billion naira relative to the 2003 budget figure of 976.2 billion naira. In 2004 when the implementation of the harmonized report of the Study and Working Groups commenced in earnest, the FIRS collection figure rose to nearly 1.2 trillion naira. The collection target set by the Federal Government for the Federal Inland Revenue Service in 2011 was 3.63 trillion naira. Actual collection was 4.62 trillion naira. This amount, which exceeded the government's target by nearly one trillion naira, represents an all time high collection figure. At 1.51 trillion naira, the non oil portion of the total collection was also an all time high. Furthermore, compared to the 2011 budget figure of 4.48 trillion naira, the 2011 collection showed a surplus of 14 billion naira relative to the national budget. While these figures are not sufficient to address the development challenges facing our country, they are improvements on past performance and an indication that with commitment on the part of all stakeholders, we can move our country forward.

The Study Group on the Nigerian tax system, which was inaugurated by the Federal Government in 2002, laid the foundation for the tax sector reforms. The recommendations of the Study Group were reviewed by a Working Group set up by the Federal Government in January 2004. The harmonized report of the two groups, which set out the reform agenda, was presented to the Federal Executive Council in October 2004. The implementation of the reform agenda involved legislative reforms; organisational restructuring, the enactment of a National Tax Policy, new funding mechanism, improved taxpayer education, improved dispute resolution mechanism, taxpayer registration, human capacity building, automation of key processes, improved refund mechanism, etc. The progress that has been recorded can be attributed, in the main, to three factors: first, determination on the part of the government to diversify the revenue base resulted in strong political support to the Service; second, focused determination on the part of the FIRS Board, Management, staff and external stakeholders (including international partners) has been crucial; lastly, investment in technology and modern work tools has also yielded significant results.

The Federal Inland Revenue Service has been in the driving seat of the reforms. The various States' Boards of Internal Revenue, under the auspices of the Joint Tax Board, have been invaluable partners on this journey. The tripartite nature of my office as Executive Chairman of the Federal Inland Revenue Service; Chairman Federal

Inland Revenue Service Board; and Chairman Joint Tax Board places me at the center of it all. Among the several milestones achieved between 2004 and now, I am particularly elated that taxation has been elevated to the front burner of national discourse. There is no better way to mobilize and sustain public consciousness in matters of civic responsibility. Several States are replicating the tax system reforms at the sub-national level with instant- and impressive-results. While counting the gains, we must also emphasise on prudence in the management of public funds. This is the only way the gains recorded can be sustained-and surpassed-in the long term.

God bless Nigeria.

Ifueko Omoigui Okauru, MFR
Executive Chairman, Federal Inland Revenue Service
Chairman, Federal Inland Revenue Service Board
Chairman, Joint Tax Board

Acknowledgements

The Service acknowledges the contributions of all its stakeholders to the on-going reforms. A compendium chronicling the various stakeholders and their respective contributions to the tax system reforms is in the works. For the moment, I want to specifically appreciate Ben Pever for his role in the production of this handbook. I also want to specially acknowledge the following people whose cooperation and contributions made the production of this handbook a reality: Mark Anthony Dike; Victor Ekundayo; Malik Tukur; B. T Abubakar; Michael Ango; Segun Sosimi; Terzungwe Atser; Ifeanyichukwu Azuka Aniyie; Michael Otubogunwa; Bala Zoakah; Chinedu Ekeh; Yemi Aladesawe; Kolawole O. O; Ogbang T. A; Ambrose Appollos Gombe; and Olusola Fowobaje.

Ifueko Omoigui Okauru
Abuja, February 2012

CHAPTER ONE

A Brief History of Taxation in Nigeria

The history of taxation in Nigeria can be categorized into three eras: pre-colonial, colonial and the post-colonial. During the pre-colonial era, taxes such as *gandu, zakkat, kudin-kasa, Jangali, shukka-shukka, gado* and *kudin sarauta* were practiced in Northern Emirates. In the South West, the *Obas* were levying taxes such as *Ishakole, Owo ode* and *Owo Asinghu*. Benin Kingdom also had an elaborate system of taxation in place which the British found on their arrival at the close of the 19th Century.

During the colonial era, the High Commissioner for Northern Nigeria, Sir Frederick Lugard reviewed the existing taxes in Northern Nigeria and decided to systemise them. This led to the passage of the *Stamp Duties Proclamation No. 8 1903* and the *Native Revenue Proclamation No. 2 1906*. Northern Nigeria was therefore, the launch pad for direct taxation in Nigeria. In 1917, following the amalgamation of the Southern and Northern Protectorates three years earlier, the 1906 Proclamation was re-styled the *Native Revenue Ordinance No. 1 1917*. The 1917 ordinance was amended in 1918 and again in

1

1927 to extend direct taxation to the Western and Eastern Provinces respectively.

Another feature of colonial taxation was the lumping of personal and business taxation under one and the same regulatory framework. The first law to separate company taxation from personal taxation was the *Companies Income Tax Ordinance No. 14 1939*. The ordinance was however repealed one year after its enactment. In 1958, the *Income Tax Administration Ordinance No. 39* established three tax administrative bodies to strengthen tax administration in the country. These were the Federal Board of Inland Revenue, the Scrutineer Committees and the Body of Appeal Commissioners. Another major milestone in taxation was recorded in 1959 with the passage of the *Petroleum Profits Ordinance No. 15 1959*. This law was necessary to regulate the taxation of income arising from petroleum operations following the discovery of oil in Oloibiri by Shell in 1956.

The first major post-colonial development in the area of taxation was the passage, in 1961, of the *Companies Income Tax Act No. 22 1961* and the *Income Tax Management Act No. 21 1961.* The regulatory framework for personal income taxation was therefore, again, separated from that of corporate income taxation for the second time, a practice that has endured to date. While

CITA 1961 regulated corporate taxation, ITMA 1961 regulated the taxation of personal income and is the precursor to the current *Personal Income Tax Act*. ITMA also created, for the first time, the Joint Tax Board with the principal objective of promoting uniform practices and procedures in personal income taxation across the Federation.

Other major developments that have taken place in the Nigerian tax system since independence include series of reform efforts by successive administrations. In 1979, the Federal Government set up a Task Force on tax administration headed by Alhaji Shehu Musa. The report of the Task Force formed the basis for the enactment of the *Companies Income Tax Act No. 28 1979* which, together with the amendments thereto, is the current legislation regulating the taxation of corporate income. In 1991, the Federal Government set up a Study Group on the Nigerian Tax System and Administration headed by Professor Emmanuel Edozien. The recommendations of the Study Group formed the basis for the promulgation of the *Finance (Miscellaneous Taxation Provisions) (Amendment) Decree No. 3 of 1993*. The decree re-structured the FBIR by establishing the FIRS as an operational arm of the Board. It also established States Boards of Internal Revenue and Local Government

Revenue Committees. Again in 1992, the Study Group on Indirect Taxation was constituted under the Chairmanship of Dr. Sylvester Ugoh. The recommendation of the Ugoh Committee formed the basis for the enactment of the Value Added Tax Act and also marked the refocusing of government's attention from direct to indirect taxation. In 2002, the Study Group on the review of the Nigerian Tax System headed by Professor Dotun Philips was constituted. The report of the Dotun Philips Study Group was reviewed by a private sector driven Working Group headed by Mr. Seyi Bickersteth. The harmonized report of the two groups provided the roadmap for the reforms that commenced in the Nigerian tax system in 2004, and have been ongoing to date.

CHAPTER TWO

Current Legislative Underpinning

The overarching legislative framework is the Constitution of the Federal Republic of Nigeria 1999, as amended. First, Section 24 (f) of the Constitution obligates every citizen of Nigeria to *"declare his income honestly to appropriate and lawful agencies and pay his tax promptly."* Second, the Constitution defines the legislative competence of each tier of government. Since there can be no tax without an enabling legislation, the definition of legislative powers by the Constitution is central in determining which tier of the Federation has jurisdiction over what taxes. The relevant provisions under the Constitution are contained in Sections 4 and the Second Schedule to the Constitution. Section 4 (1) vests the legislative powers of the Federal Republic in the National Assembly while Section 4 (7) vests the legislative powers of the 36 States of the Federation in their respective Houses of Assembly. The delimitation of these powers is such that a House of Assembly of a State cannot legislate on any item on the Exclusive Legislative List contained in Part I to the Second Schedule of the Constitution. The States can, however, legislate on items on the Concurrent List contained in Part II to the Second Schedule; but again Section 4 (5) places a caveat to the extent that where a State law is inconsistent with a Federal law, the Federal law prevails and the State law is null and void to the extent of its inconsistency.

The tax items specifically listed on the Exclusive List are: *customs and excise duties*: (item 16) *export duties*: (item 25) *stamp duties*: (item 58) and *taxation of incomes, profits and capital gains*: (item 59). The Concurrent List contains no specific tax types in respect of which States may legislate. This is not to suggest that the States do not possess legislative competence in relation to tax matters. In addition to the powers vested in the States Houses of Assembly in Section 4 (7) *"to make laws for the peace, order and good government of the States"*; paragraph 9 of the Second Schedule empowers a State House of Assembly to make a tax law and in doing so, require a Local Government Council in the State to collect the tax so prescribed. Furthermore, paragraph 10 provides that in delegating tax collection powers to a Local Government under paragraph 9; the law passed by the House of Assembly must regulate liability to the tax in a manner that would ensure the tax is not levied on the same taxpayer by more than one Local Government Council. The combined import of Section 4 (7) and paragraphs 9 and 10 of Part II to the Second Schedule is that States possess *residual* tax jurisdiction in exercise whereof, the States may delegate the responsibility to *collect* to the Local Governments.

It must be pointed out that under the doctrine of "covering the field" which is codified under Section 4 (5) of the Constitution; the power of the State to legislate on residual matters is subject to the Federal power to legislate. This scenario is best captured in the regulation of the value added tax, VAT. VAT is neither on the Exclusive nor Concurrent Legislative List; making it a "residual" matter which ordinarily should fall within the purview of State legislative competence. However, since the Value Added Tax Act, which is a federal law has already covered the field of consumption tax; any law passed by a State Assembly that is identical to VAT is null and void in the light of Section 4 (5) of the Constitution. The Court of Appeal reiterated this position in the case of **Attorney General of Lagos State Vs Eko Hotels Ltd and Federal Board of Inland Revenue 1 TLRN 198.**

While the 1999 Constitution defines the legislative competence of each tier of the government, the Taxes and Levies (Approved List for Collection) Act Cap T2 Laws of the Federation of Nigeria (LFN) 2004 defines the jurisdiction of the three tiers of government in terms of actual collection of the various tax types. For the FIRS, this includes: the Petroleum Profits Tax; Companies Income Tax; Personal Income Tax (FCT residents, non-residents, members of the Nigerian Police and the Armed Forces, employees of the Federal Ministry of Foreign Affairs); Withholding tax on companies, residents of the FCT and non-residents; Capital Gains Tax (corporations, FCT residents and non-residents); Stamp Duties (corporations and FCT residents); Tertiary Education Tax and Value Added Tax.

In addition to the taxes specifically defined in the Taxes and Levies (Approved List for Collection) Act, the National Information Technology Development Act 2007 empowers the Federal Inland Revenue Service to administer the National Information Technology Development Levy imposed by section 12 of the Act. Lastly, the Federal Inland Revenue Service (Establishment) Act 2007 empowers the Service to administer all fees, levies and taxes relating to Oil Exploration License, Oil Mining License, Oil Production License, royalties and rents.

CHAPTER THREE

Reforms to the Tax System

The Federal Inland Revenue Service, working with and as an integral part of the Joint Tax Board, has been in the driving seat of the reforms arising from the recommendations of the Study and Working Groups. In this regard, the Service has also initiated several reforms towards modernising its structures and processes with the view of enhancing effectiveness and efficiency in tax administration. Some of the achievements to date are in the following areas:

a. Developing a tax reform agenda
b. Enactment/Amendment of Tax laws
c. National Tax Policy
d. Articulating a clear direction for the Service and the JTB
e. Improved Funding
f. Reengineering and Automation of Key Processes
g. Reorganisation of the Service towards a modern tax authority
h. Job Creation
i. Career/Skill Development

j. Improved Remuneration/Welfare/Working Environment

k. Audit

l. Investigation

m. Enforcement

n. Tax Payer Education

o. Communication and Liaison

p. Dispute Resolution

q. Tax Refund System

r. Performance Management

s. Inter-Agency Collaboration

t. Gazetting of regulations/orders.

a. *Development of harmonised Tax Reform Agenda* The Study Group on the Nigerian Tax System under the chairmanship of Professor Dotun Phillips was inaugurated by then Finance Minister Mallam Adamu Ciroma on 6 August 2002 with an eleven-item terms of reference that were all tailored at repositioning the tax system for better efficiency. The Study Group submitted its report in July 2003. A Working Group chaired by KPMG's Seyi Bickersteth was inaugurated on 12 January 2004 by Finance Minister Dr. Ngozi Okonjo-Iweala. The terms of reference of the Working Group were to evaluate the recommendations of the Study Group; prioritise the set of strategies required to reform the tax system; and segment the strategies to be implemented into short term (six months); medium term (two years); and long term (five years). The Working Group submitted its report to the Federal Government in March 2004. While there were some areas of divergence between the report of the Working Group and that of the Study Group, both reports agreed on the objective of the reform which was, and still is, to diversify the revenue base of the government beyond oil and oil related sources. Furthermore, both report agreed on most of the fundamentals required to achieve that objective. Under the auspices of the Open Society Initiative, the reports of the two Groups were further exposed to a wide range of stakeholders including but not limited to tax consultants, the IMF Mission on Tax Administration, the Federal Ministry of Finance, the Economic Management Team, and the Management of the Federal Inland Revenue Service. Stakeholder inputs were incorporated where appropriate, into the tax reform document and by August 2004, the Federal Inland Revenue Service had distilled a roadmap for the implementation of the reforms. At the Extraordinary Session of the Federal Executive Council Meeting held on 18 October 2004, the Executive Chairman of the Federal Inland Revenue Service outlined the reform agenda to the Federal Executive Council. The Council identified three broad, critical strategies required to implement the harmonised tax reform agenda. These were autonomy for the Federal Inland Revenue Service; increased funding for the Service; and amendment to the various tax laws. The Council therefore, approved that the Service should be granted autonomy in the areas of recruitment, funding and remuneration. A four percent cost of collection of non oil taxes (which was subsequently codified in the FIRS Establishment Act 2007) was also approved and provided for in the 2005 Appropriation Bill. Finally, the Council constituted a Presidential Technical Committee under the chairmanship of the Attorney General of the Federation to draft a bill that would give effect to the legislative changes required to actualise the reform objectives.

b.   *Enactment/Amendment of Tax Laws*

Some aspects of the reform agenda could not be implemented without legislative reforms. While the original concept at the time of inaugurating the Presidential Technical Committee (PTC) was to come up with a bill that would address all the legal changes required; the Legal Sub-committee of the PTC in the course of its work determined that issues pertaining to tax administration should be addressed in a Bill establishing the Federal Inland Revenue Service while other issues should be addressed by amendments to existing legislations. Altogether, the Committee presented nine tax bills to the Federal Government and in November 2005, the bills were forwarded as Executive Bills to the National

Assembly. Four of the bills were signed into law in April 2007. These were:

a)   FIRS Establishment Act, 2007: The Federal Inland Revenue Service (Establishment) Act 2007 has addressed some of the problems identified by the Study and Working Groups as impeding effective tax administration in the country. These include autonomy and secure funding for the FIRS; new governance structure for the FIRS; increased powers for the FIRS and its Board; improved mechanism for tax refund; improved mechanism for dispute resolution; and increased sanctions and penalties for infractions against tax laws.

b)   Value Added Tax (Amendment) Act, 2007: The Value Added Tax (Amendment) Act has introduced better clarity in the administration of value added tax by removing ambiguous provisions in the principal Act. The amendment Act has also strengthened enforcement provisions; introduces the principle of derivation in the sharing of VAT revenue; confers, for the first time, agency status on companies in the oil and gas sector; and introduces a Third Schedule to the principal Act containing zero rated goods and services.

c)   National Automotive Council (Amendment) Act, 2007: In line with the desire to streamline the number of taxes which constitute more nuisance than revenue value, the

National Automotive Council (Amendment) Act 2007 abolished the automotive council levy of 2% of Cost Insurance and Freight, CIF, value of all imported vehicles. The amendment further provides that the Council should henceforth be funded through appropriation.

d)   Companies Income Tax (Amendment) Act, 2007: In the light of the provisions of the FIRS Establishment Act, certain provisions such as those relating to the Federal Board of Inland Revenue and the Body of Appeal Commissioners were no longer relevant and were consequently deleted by the Companies Income Tax (Amendment) Act 2007. The amendment Act also brings clarity to hitherto ambiguous provisions; closes loopholes in the law; makes self assessment mandatory; transfers the power to vary tax rates from the President to the National Assembly; removes the limitation hitherto placed on companies from carrying losses forward; increases the threshold for donations to tertiary and research institutions; and increases sanctions and penalties for infractions against tax laws.

The passage of the four Bills in 2007 left five other Bills outstanding. In this category, two were passed and signed into law in 2011 while one is currently being reworked. These are:

a)   The Tertiary Education Trust Fund (Establishment; etc) Act 2011: The original proposal of the PTC was to abolish education tax and restructure the Education Fund to be financed through budgetary allocation and other sources. However, the Tertiary Education Trust Fund (Establishment) Act 2011 does not abolish education tax; rather, it repealed the Education Tax Act along with the Education Fund and creates in its place, the Tertiary Education Trust Fund with special focus on the development of tertiary education in Nigeria. The major difference introduced by the Act as passed is that primary and secondary educational institutions no longer benefit the 30 percent and 20 percent respectively of education tax proceeds as was the case under the Education Tax Act. The entire Fund is now dedicated to the development of tertiary education in Nigeria and accordingly, the tax is now named the tertiary education tax.

b)   The Personal Income Tax (Amendment) Act 2011: The Personal Income Tax (Amendment) Act was passed by the House of Representatives on the 25th May 2011; the Senate on 1st June 2011 and assented to by President Jonathan on 14th June 2011. The hallmarks of the amendment Act include the reduction of tax burden through introduction of a Consolidated Relief Allowance; the widening of tax base through the provision of presumptive tax regime and self assessment; provision of clarity through the removal of ambiguous terms and provisions; improvement of dispute resolution mechanism; enhanced operational capacity for tax authorities; and stiffer penalties for infractions against the Act.

c)   The Petroleum Profits Tax (Amendment) Bill: The objectives of the proposed amendments to the Petroleum Profits Tax Act were to streamline incentives in the oil and gas sector; raise the threshold for donations to tertiary and research institutions; introduce transparency in the petroleum sector and provide for stiffer penalties for offenders. The Petroleum Profits Tax (Amendment) Bill was subsequently subsumed into the Petroleum Industry Bill (PIB) and is being reworked in collaboration with other agencies of government. The PIB was originally sponsored at the behest of industry players in the petroleum sector to address the problems associated with the sector. The PIB is therefore, an amalgam of the original provisions as contained under that name as well as the proposed amendments to the PPTA which were the result of issues arising from audits conducted internally as part of the tax reform agenda as well as issues arising from audits conducted by the Nigeria Extractive Industry Initiative (NEITI). It seeks to replace the existing myriad of legislative instruments and institutional organs governing the petroleum industry. When eventually passed, it will enthrone a system that is regimented by an omnibus legislation that establishes clear rules and procedures for the administration of the petroleum industry in Nigeria.

Out of the nine original Bills submitted in November 2005, the Customs and Excise Tariffs Act (Amendment) Bill and the National Sugar Development Council Act (Amendment) Bill were not attended to. The two Bills were meant to address the same objective as the National Automotive Council (Amendment) Act, 2007, namely, the streamlining of levies of doubtful revenue value.

Furthermore, the Service is currently working with the IMF Fiscal Department on another wave of legal reforms. The current initiative is aimed at achieving three major objectives. First, to achieve simplicity of language, enhance understanding of tax laws and reduce compliance and enforcement cost; all existing tax laws are being reworked and recaptured in simple, plain English that is devoid of ambiguous and complex terms. Second, in line with global best practice, the statutory framework for tax administration is to be separated from the framework for imposing tax and sanctions. Therefore, tax administration provisions in all current tax laws are being excised and consolidated into a proposed Tax Administration Bill while all provisions relating to assessment and collection will be contained in a separate Income Tax Code. The Capital Gains Tax Act will however, not be consolidated alongside other income tax laws into the Income Tax Bill but rather; it will be incorporated into the Petroleum Industry Bill which is envisaged to remain a stand-alone statutory framework for the regulation of petroleum operations, given the specialised nature of the oil and gas sector. Another statutory framework that is envisaged to be a stand-alone legislation is the Value Added Tax Act. The third objective is to harmonise the functions and roles of all Federal revenue collecting agencies. A Jointly Collectible Taxes of the Federation Bill is being proposed for this purpose.

c.   *The National Tax Policy*
Both the Study and Working Groups addressed macro and micro issues in tax policy and administration in the country and made appropriate recommendations. The two Groups agreed that it was desirable to have in place a national policy platform that would prescribe principles and also outline the objectives that will govern the practice of taxation in Nigeria at all times; a framework by which all stakeholders must subscribe and to which they will be held accountable. In July 2005, a Presidential Technical Committee was inaugurated to drive the harmonized recommendations of the Study and Working Groups on the National Tax Policy and to develop the background to the document. The Committee in addition to developing the background document also made sensitisation visits

around the six geo-political zones of Nigeria to seek inputs from a wide spectrum of stakeholders. Stakeholders' inputs were incorporated into the draft document as appropriate. The draft National Tax Policy was presented to, and adopted by the Federal Executive Council on 20th January 2010. Following approval by the Federal Executive Council on Wednesday, 20th February, 2010, the National Tax Policy document was then presented by the Honourable Minister of Finance to the National Economic Council on 9th March, 2010 to guarantee national acceptability and implementation in the country. The policy is a blueprint specifying the guidelines, rules and standards necessary to make the country's tax system globally competitive and in the process, diversify the economy by making taxes the major source of government revenue.

d.   *Articulation of a Clear Strategic Direction*
The FIRS Strategic Plan 2004-2007 was a new threshold in medium term strategic planning for the Service. The framework agreed on the Vision, Mission, Values and Goals that would drive the activities of the Service and the key performance indicators by which performance would be measured. This Plan is now being reviewed towards the adoption of a Tax System Vision 2020 to be articulated in collaboration with the Joint Tax Board. The FIRS Tax System Vision 2020 aligns with the Vision 20:2020

national development agenda. The FIRS Vision is to be driven by three strategic components which are long term plans (2020); four-year medium term plans (the current one being the FIRS Medium Term Plan 2012-2015) and short term plan (FIRS Annual Corporate Plans).

e.   *Improved Funding of the Service*

Prior to 2005, the Service was funded just like any other agency of the Federal Government. In 2005, a new funding mechanism based on "cost of collection" was approved for the Service. This mechanism was codified two years later under Section 15 of the FIRS Establishment Act 2007. Under this new funding system, a certain percentage of non oil taxes collected by the Service is appropriated by the National Assembly for the execution of the Service's major expenditure sub-heads: Personnel, Recurrent and Capital. The new funding method has enhanced the ability of the Service to recruit and pay for the appropriate complement of staff; acquire assets, equipments, machinery and tools; and invest in the requisite technology necessary to modernize the operations of the Service. Overall, improved funding has enabled the Service collect more revenues for the government.

f. Modernisation of the Service/Re-engineering and Automation of key processes

A major flank in the achievement of set vision and mission is the automation of key processes. As at date, at least 20 modernisation projects have been embarked on, concluded or at different stages of completion. Some of the major projects are described below:

a) Automation of Collection: The manual collection process in place before the advent of reforms was fraught with leakages that undermined the integrity of the entire process. The central objective of the automation project was to create a system that would ensure that funds collected are not delayed, converted or diverted. In July 2004, the FIRS Bank Collection Reform Committee was inaugurated. The committee consisted of representatives of the Federal Inland Revenue Service; Central Bank of Nigeria; Office of the Accountant General of the Federation; Nigerian Customs Service; Telnet (Nigeria) Limited InterSwitch Limited and four competitively and provisionally selected Lead Banks. The Committee was able to identify limitations of the current system; leakage areas; areas of process improvement; skill gaps and requirements; and infrastructure requirements. The project, which was tagged Project FACT (Friendly, Accurate, Complete and Timely) commenced pilot runs in five tax offices on 22 November 2005. This was followed up with necessary surveys, documentations and quality test runs. On 24 April 2006, Project FACT was rolled out as the new collection system of the FIRS. The automation process ensures that taxes are collected by designated "collecting banks" and the proceeds are transmitted within 24 hours to one of the four "lead banks." The lead banks in turn ensure that FIRS payments from all parts of the country are swept electronically into the Central Bank of Nigeria within two days. This has largely addressed the issue of trapped funds in banks and reduced fraud in the collection system. Automation gives the Federal Government real time, almost minute by minute report on taxes collected by the FIRS. Many States Boards of Internal Revenue have adopted automated bank payment process for tax collections. Banks are selected and taxpayers pay through these banks and are issued electronic tickets as evidence of payment through the bank. This process helps the Boards to reduce or eliminate leakages and determine at any given time the quantum and position of tax funds. FIRS and some SBIRs are on the Interswitch payment platform while other SBIRs are either on E-Tranzact or Chams switch platforms. Some SBIRs have automated their receipt issuance to check the incidence of fake receipts while some have automated their Tax Clearance Certificate issuance. The FIRS has introduced the use of electronic worksheets and mandatory use of TIN for payment of WHT and this has significantly increased the tax take.

b)   The Integrated Tax Administration System (ITAS): As
part of the Tax System Vision 2020, the Service resolved
to establish a tax operation that is driven by a robust and
cost effective Integrated Tax Administration System. As a
corollary to this, the 2008–2011 Medium Term Plan has as
one of its objectives, the complete implementation of the
ITAS Project, inclusive of document and records
management systems. The Project received a major boost
in 2010 with the endorsement of the Federal Executive
Council (FEC) and approval for the funding of the project.
Following FEC approval, the contract was signed in
September 2011 and full implementation of the Project is
expected be achieved within three years while post
implementation support services will run for two years
from date of delivery.

c)   Taxpayers Identification Number (TIN) Program: Real
time data and information is the live wire of any tax
agency. In 2008, in discharging its responsibility to issue
taxpayer identification numbers, the FIRS commenced a
process of assigning taxpayer identification numbers to
tax payers within its jurisdiction. As at 31st December 2011,
the total number of registered taxpayers on the TIN project
was 851,456. This number consists of 437,885 corporate
entities, 169,263 individuals in business and 244,308
individuals in employment. To consolidate on this and
truly issue **unique** taxpayer numbers nationwide in

collaboration with state tax authorities, the Joint Tax Board (made up of the Federal Inland Revenue Service and the 36 State Boards of Internal Revenue (SBIRs)) initiated a unique TIN program to uniquely identify and register taxpayers nationwide using ten fingers biometrics for individual taxpayers. The objectives of the TIN program are to:

i. Have reliable and centralized information on all taxpayers in the country; making it easy for information sharing among all tax authorities, thereby deepening the tax base.

ii. Create the platform for effective tax administration that operates on reliable taxpayer registration and effective tracking of taxpayers

iii. Automate taxpayer registration activities at all levels of government and therefore facilitate a sustainable platform for revenue generation

iv. Eliminate multiple taxpayer registration through the creation and management of a central taxpayer database

v. Reduce, on the part of tax authorities, the administrative costs associated with manual taxpayer registration and on the part of taxpayers the delays associated with processing requests or status reports. Overall, the TIN will engender confidence and increase voluntary compliance.

vi. Widen the tax base through the registration of all eligible taxpayers.

vii. Provide a reliable tool for national planning, budgeting and allocation of resources.

g. Reorganisation of the Service towards a modern tax authority and improved taxpayer focus

The structural reorganization of the FIRS occurred at two broad levels. The first level of the reorganisation was the conversion of offices from the basis of tax type to taxpayer need. This saw the integration of area tax offices with VAT offices thereby creating one-stop-shop for taxpayers. Under the old system, Area Tax Offices handled income tax matters while Value Added Tax offices handled VAT matters. The Integrated Tax Offices that have resulted from the merger of Area Tax Offices and VAT offices made away with this dichotomy. On the part of taxpayers, this has reduced the cost of compliance as taxpayers are no longer required to visit different locations to carry out transactions. All the Integrated Tax Offices are mandated to handle all types of tax transactions. On the part of tax officials, it has provided an opportunity for all field officers to be rounded professionals in all types of operations as opposed to the erstwhile practice where officers in VAT offices were not versed in processes or procedures in Area Tax Offices and *vice versa*.

Still laying emphasis on taxpayer need, the second level of organisational restructuring also witnessed the segmentation of offices to focus on categories of taxpayers classified along the lines of small, medium and large taxpayers. Different threshold have been created for each category and departments created to cater for the operations of each segment. In addition, new structures have been created where necessary to offer support services to the core mandate of tax collection. In this regard, units have either been upgraded or entire new departments created to fill these needs. In 2007, the Service introduced a "group system" structure where all departments and units within the organisation are grouped together on the basis of functions and responsibilities, under any of five groups namely the Tax Operations Group (TOG); the Corporate Development Group (CDG); the Compliance and Enforcement Group (CEG); the Support Services Group (SSG) and the Chairman's Office Group (COG). The groups are headed by Coordinating Directors while the departments within the groups are headed by directors. Organisational key performance indicators flow from the Executive Chairman of the Service to the groups and cascade down the line to departments, units and individuals. Organisational change continues to be dynamic to align with the plans of the Service.

Recognising the evolution of the Service overtime, there is a proposal to further change the structure effective March 2012 into the following focal groups:

a) Modernisation
b) Field Operations
c) Standards and Compliance
d) Support Services; and
e) Executive Chairman's Direct Reports

h. *Job Creation*

As a result of the reorganization and realignment of functions, over 3,000 new job openings in specific skill driven areas were created. These openings were first filled in 2010 through a competitive recruitment exercise with a view to filling the gaps by 2012. The FIRS Board raised the standard for entry into the Service to a minimum of first degree or Higher National Diploma. In order not to foreclose the employees of the erstwhile Federal Board of Inland Revenue whose qualifications fell short of the new entry requirements from transiting into the new Federal Inland Revenue Service, the Management of the Service and the staff unions signed a memorandum of understanding granting a grace period of up to 2013 to employees whose qualifications fell short of the new requirement to upgrade themselves.

i.   *Career/Skill Development*

Professionalism is one of the core values that drive the strategic operations of the Service. The premium placed on professionalism by the Management of the Service led to the introduction of six career paths along which every employee may progress in the course of service. These career paths include Tax, Legal, General Administration, Human Resources, Finance and Information Technology. There is also a parallel career path for technical persons on such assignments as driving and maintenance. All actions pertaining to an officer of the Service are driven by the requirements and needs of his career path. Over 5,000 management, manager and officer cadre (out of the current 6,120 staff in place), have enjoyed specialized and industry/issue specific training and Study Tours, within and outside the country in the last three years. Hitherto, very little training was in place. Most staff had received no training for over 10 years. To address this trend, the capacity building function was enhanced by a clear focus on learning and development to deliver qualitative, functional and professional development of staff, and support their ability to deliver the Service's mandate at all times; and to also equip staff to meet the challenges associated with delivering that mandate in terms of value, culture, professional and personal development. The training philosophy of the Service is to provide structured and systematic training that enables employees to acquire the skills, knowledge and qualifications relevant to their development for the realisation of their career potentials in the Service.

j.   *Improved Remuneration/Welfare/Working Environment*

There has been considerable improvement in staff remuneration with the new salary scheme approved by the National Salaries and Wages Commission effective April 2007. In 2009, quarterly performance bonuses were introduced for any officer/department that attained the required benchmark of performance targets for the quarter. Loans were given to staff to purchase houses during the sale of Federal Government houses. In July 2011, another upward review of salaries was done with the approval of the Commission. Also, in 2011, the Management approved a Housing and Car Loans Scheme for eligible staff of the Service. Various forms of assistance have also been rendered by the Management of the Service to the FIRS Multi-Purpose Cooperative Society to the benefit of staff.

In addition to these welfare schemes, new emphasis has been placed on the creation of a conducive work-place environment. In this regard, all offices of the services have been modernised or in the process of being modernised. New offices acquired while others are under construction.

The Facility, Security and Safety Management Department is to ensure adequate standards of comfort, convenience, security and safety of staff, visitors and assets of the Service.

k.   *Audit*

The Service had a Tax Audit Unit prior to the reforms but the structure and function of the unit was considered inadequate at the onset of the reforms. Tax audit, especially of the large tax payers, was identified as one of the seven strategic flanks of the FIRS Modernisation Plan. The ball was set rolling with the establishment in February 2005, of the first set of operational audit units in the five Large Tax Offices. This was the first step towards replicating audit functions in all FIRS tax offices. In addition, to ensure adequate standards of audit are set and effectively monitored, the Tax Audit, Processes and Programmes Department, TAPPD was created. TAPPD is responsible for the design of audit policies, programmes and processes as well as the monitoring of field auditors.

l.   *Investigation*

The erstwhile Investigation department in the Service was strengthened with the resulting tax investigation department as one of the direct reports to the Executive Chairman. The Department is responsible for investigating tax evasion, fraud and other infractions of tax laws and is manned by special purpose tax officers as provided in the FIRSEA 2007, to provide support to field tax offices.

m. *Enforcement*

Enforcement has been weak and continually requires strengthening. The FIRSEA 2007 provides clear and additional enforcement powers to the Service. In defining the functions of each of the field tax offices, the filing and debt enforcement unit was set up as one of the integral functions of the tax office. It is expected that these units will with time increase the effectiveness of enforcement action. To support these units, the Legal Department at the Headquarters identifies cases for prosecution and also prosecutes cases referred to it. As an added focus on enforcement, a debt enforcement and special prosecution unit was also setup to focus on the top 100 corporations and MDAs (Ministries, Departments and Agencies).

n. *Taxpayer Education*

Taxpayer education is one of the strategic flank of the Tax Reform Agenda. At the onset of the reforms, the IMF Focused Visitation Mission Report identified taxpayer education service as a major area within the Nigerian tax system that needed intervention by way of reform. The conduct of taxpayer education prior to the reforms was not adequate to promote voluntary compliance which is a key attribute of a modern, robust and vibrant tax system. After several permutations aimed at improving tax payer education, the Service finally rested with the creation in April 2011 of the Taxpayer Service Policy, Process and Programmes Department to drive all policies, programmes and processes relating to taxpayer education services.

o.   *Communication and Liaison*
Between 2004 and now, corporate communication has been carried out using different platforms and media. These include the use of a television awareness programme called Tax Matters; publications such as the Gauge Magazine – a quarterly newsletter, the monthly news bulletin, meetings with staff and stakeholder sessions amongst others.

The Service is liaising with the Federal Ministry of Education to introduce taxation as a study course at all levels of education in a bid to institutionalise taxation as an integral part of our national culture. Furthermore, in pursuance of its commitment to taxpayer education and the mainstreaming of tax curriculum into the Nigerian educational system to build a pipeline of future tax officers as well as prospective taxpayers, the Service in collaboration with the National Universities Commission, NUC, has developed a curriculum for the take-off of the FIRS Professorial Chairs in Taxation, which at this initial stage, is targeted at masters and PhD degrees in Accounting and Law with special bias in taxation. The key objective of the FIRS Professorial Chairs in Taxation is to build a pipeline of taxpayers and tax compliant stakeholders. Other objectives include developing tax curriculum in selected Nigerian universities at both undergraduate and postgraduate levels; improving related infrastructure for the teaching of taxation courses and research on global taxation trends, developments and best practices; and providing scholarships for the study of taxation in selected universities. The University of Abuja was selected alongside 12 other universities; two from each of the six geopolitical zones for the endowment. Another criterion for the selection was to ensure that in each geopolitical zone one Federal and one State university were selected. The selected universities are in the process of domesticating the curriculum and also engaging professors for the chairs.

The Service has also collaborated with Society for Youth Empowerment in Nigeria (SYEN) since 2008 in a partnership that has seen the establishment of tax clubs in post primary schools under the name Students Advocates for Tax, SAT. The main objective of the partnership is to bring future taxpayers into the tax net by "catching them young." This has led to the establishment by the FIRS of the Students Tax Advocate Initiative (STAI) to drive advocacy amongst the youth in collaboration with SYEN and other Non-Governmental Organisations (NGOs) in a focussed manner.

Finally, through the practice of corporate social responsibility, the Service seeks to build trust and confidence among stakeholders. In this regard, the Service has purchased and donated books, computers and other teaching aids to schools; and also funded several charitable and social spirited projects.

p.   *Dispute Resolution*

Until the passage of the Federal Inland Revenue Service Establishment Act 2007, two mechanisms existed as points of first contact in the resolution of tax disputes. These were the Body of Appeal Commissioners and the Value Added Tax Tribunal. While the former handled all disputes between the Service and taxpayers arising from the administration of income taxes, the latter handled disputes arising from the administration of value added tax. The Federal Inland Revenue Establishment Act 2007 establishes the Tax Appeal Tribunal which replaces and combines the functions of the erstwhile Body of Appeal Commissioners and the Value Added Tax Tribunal. The TAT provides a one-stop shop for taxpayers to seek redress if dissatisfied with the decision by the revenue authority. Further appeals from the TAT lie to the Federal High Court, and from there to the Court of Appeal and the Supreme Court respectively. The Tax Appeal Tribunal was inaugurated by the Finance Minister on 5 February 2010. The Tribunal has eight zones namely Abuja, Lagos, North East, North West, North Central, South East, South West and South-South zones. The jurisdiction of the Tribunal is in respect of disputes arising from assessment under all tax legislations administered by the Service as contained in the First Schedule of the FIRS Establishment Act. In addition, Section 14 of the Personal Income Tax (Amendment) Act 2011 provides that all disputes arising from personal income tax shall be heard by the Tax Appeal Tribunal.

q.   *Tax Refund System*

The delay associated with the tax refund process hitherto has been addressed by Section 23 of the FIRS Establishment Act 2007. The section has created mechanisms to ensure that taxpayers who are over-assessed receive tax refunds due to them. The first obligation of the Service is to ensure that established claims are refunded within 90 days of the decision of the Service to refund. Second, Section 23(4) requires the Accountant-General of the Federation to open a dedicated account into which funds appropriated by the National Assembly specifically for refund purposes shall be maintained and administered by the Service. The tax refund application must be initiated by the taxpayer and directed to the concerned tax office stating the exact reason for the refund, the period of the transaction, the FIRS receipt of payment, bank tellers, print out of record of Paydirect/web portal, and stamped documents if the refund pertains to stamp duties. The concerned Integrated Tax Office – Large, Medium or Micro and Small Tax Office, will forward the aforementioned documents and a Remittance Schedule to the Headquarters of the Service, following which the refund is paid to the taxpayer. The strengthening of the refund mechanism is aimed at promoting taxpayer confidence in the tax system.

r.   *Performance Management*

FIRS Annual Corporate Plans usually contain financial and non-financial targets for the relevant year. Key performance indicators, KPIs, have been introduced as benchmarking tools in order to assess and evaluate performance. KPIs are set at the corporate level and cascaded down to departmental and individual levels in accordance with the SMART acronym: Specific, Measurable, Achievable, Realistic/Rewardable, and Timely. In order to ensure optimal performance among staff, the FIRS Management introduced the quarterly performance bonus by way of one month extra salary for officers and departments that attain a certain threshold of the key performance targets. This is in recognition that it is individual performance that adds up to organisational success.

s. *Interagency Collaboration*

The FIRS is working to ensure linkages with relevant federal agencies including but not limited to the Corporate Affairs Commission (CAC)- for registered companies and organizations, the Central Bank of Nigeria (CBN)- for bank customer data, the Nigeria Deposit Insurance Corporation (NDIC)- for updates on bank reports, the Department of Petroleum Resources (DPR)- for information on all licensed companies in the downstream and upstream sectors, the National Petroleum Investment Management Services (NAPIMS) and Oil and Gas Companies- for contract awards, the Crude Oil Marketing Department of the NNPC (COMD)- for shipping companies, shipping and marketing agents in the sale of Government's crude oil equity, the Nigerian Maritime Authority (NMA) and the National Ports Authority (NPA)- for export information, the Nigerian Stock Exchange (NSE) and the Central Securities Clearing Scheme (CSCS)- for stockbroker's daily transactions, the Securities and Exchange Commission (SEC)- for public offers and private placements, the Bureau for Public Enterprises (BPE)- for information on divestments of interests in companies and corporations, the Due Process Office for Federal Government's contract awards, the Nigeria Customs Service (NCS), the Economic and Financial Crimes Commission (EFCC), Nigeria Police Force and the Nigerian Financial Intelligence Unit (NFIU) to name a few relevant agencies. Memoranda of Understanding are being signed to institutionalize such arrangements once agreed upon.

t.   *Gazetting of Regulations/Orders*

As part of the process of ensuring clarity in the interpretation and administration of tax laws, the following regulations have been put in place:

a)   *Self-Assessment Regulations*: The FIRS Management inaugurated a Self-Assessment Project Team on 3 March 2011 and charged it with the primary responsibility of developing a detailed self-assessment implementation plan to be used across all offices of the Service. Since inauguration, the Project Team has undertaken study visits to selected countries identified to have efficient self-assessment procedures. The Team further revised the risk profiling criteria and also developed Draft Self-Assessment Regulations; Draft Self-Assessment Handbook; and Draft Self-Assessment Forms. The implementation of 100 percent self-assessment is to be commenced in three FIRS offices namely Large Tax Office (Oil and Gas) Lagos, Large Tax Office (Non-Oil and Gas) Lagos and Ikeja Integrated Tax Office. The successful implementation of these three pilot projects will provide useful lessons towards the complete roll out of the project Service-wide.

b) *Orders*: Section 25 (4) (c) of the Companies Income Tax Act provides that donations made to any Fund, Body or Institution listed in the Fifth Schedule to the Act shall be allowable deduction for the purpose of ascertaining the tax liability of a company in any assessment year. Prior to the issuance of the "Amendment to the Companies Income Tax Act Order No. 1 of 2011" the eligibility of any Fund, Body or Institution to receive tax deductible donations was based on the listing of such Funds, Bodies and Institutions in the Fifth Schedule to the Act, which was done at the discretion of the Finance Minister, within the narrow requirements prescribed in the Act. The Order has widened the criteria by establishing a generic basis for determining the eligibility of such Funds, Bodies and Institutions. This has done away with the old discretionary system investing the Minister with powers to determine which Fund, Body or Institution was eligible. Further to the Order, therefore, the "Requirements for the Funds, Bodies and Institutions (under the Fifth Schedule to the Companies and Income Tax Act) Regulations 2011" have been issued spelling out the criteria for eligibility of companies to receive tax deductible donations under the Fifth Schedule to the Companies Income Tax Act. This measure further demonstrates the commitment of the Government and the Service in creating an equitable and taxpayer friendly system that is founded on transparency and a clearly defined set of rules.

In addition, the Service is currently working on putting in place the following regulations:

i.   Presumptive Tax Regulations: The Personal Income Tax Amendment Act 2011 empowers the Finance Minister to issue Regulations for the purpose of providing guidelines on the presumptive tax regime. The Presumptive Tax Regulations are intended to outline the criteria for arriving at the liability of persons whose income cannot be firmly ascertained. The Technical Committee of the FIRS Board has constituted a Working Group to produce Draft Presumptive Tax Regulations for the Minister's approval.

ii.   Taxpayer Identification Number Regulations: The TIN Regulations are intended to provide the framework for the operation of the Taxpayer Identification Number, TIN. The TIN Project Office which is situated within the Secretariat of the Joint Tax Board working in collaboration with the external Project Adviser obtained similar Regulations from other jurisdictions in order to review the precedents and adapt the contents to the Nigerian context. The TIN Project Office worked with the Legal Department of the FIRS to come up with a first draft which was exposed to the Legal Advisers of the 36 States Boards of Internal Revenue at a workshop in August 2011. Following the inputs of the 36 States into the Regulations, a national workshop is slated for February 2012 where the second draft will be exposed to a wider spectrum of stakeholders to include labour unions; Ministries, Departments and Agencies of Government; professional bodies; the Chartered Institute of Taxation of Nigeria etc for their buy-in and input towards the production of the final draft for Ministerial approval.

iii. Personal Income Tax Regulations: While the Personal Income Tax Act Amendment Act 2011 has addressed a number of loopholes in the principal Act, some provisions in the amendment Act itself have been generating debates among taxpayers. For example, the amendment Act introduces the Consolidated Relief Allowance but does not expressly delete Section 3 (1) (b) of the principal Act relating to tax free allowances. Also, there is a seeming contradiction between the mode of calculating the Consolidated Relief Allowance as contained in Section 5 of the amendment Act and paragraph (1) of the Sixth Schedule. In order to provide clarity on these and several other issues of concern to taxpayers, the FIRS has produced a Draft Personal Income Tax Regulations for the Minister's approval. When issued, the Regulations will clarify the contentious issues regarding the administration of personal income tax.

iv. *Holding Company Regulations:* In furtherance to the bank sector reforms, the Central Bank of Nigeria issued the Regulation on the Scope of Banking Activities and Ancillary Matters in 2010. The Regulations repealed the Universal Banking Licence issued to banks hitherto and also streamlined all banks into three categories namely merchant; commercial and specialised banks. Furthermore, all banks that were involved in other non banking businesses are required to divest from such businesses and as an alternative measure; restructure appropriately using the holding company model. The restructuring required to give effect to the CBN policy involves, among other things, the devolution or transfer of assets among the holding companies and their subsidiaries. From the tax point of view, the restructuring has thrown up issues such as the commencement and cessation rule; stamp duties; capital gains; withholding tax on dividends etc between the holding companies and subsidiaries. In order to address the extant issues in the banking sector and also provide a framework on similar issues that may arise in other sectors; the FIRS in the exercise of its power under Section 61 of the FIRS Establishment Act 2007 is working on a draft Information Circular that would provide guidelines on the operations of holding companies.

v. *Transfer Pricing Regulations:* Transfer pricing involves the system of setting prices for the transfer of goods, services and intangibles between or among related parties operating in more than one tax jurisdiction. It is an arrangement which companies within a conglomerate, especially multinationals, have used over time to perfect tax avoidance schemes. The Regulations being developed are intended to provide a framework for addressing tax issues arising from transactions among related parties.

CHAPTER FOUR

Revenue accruing to Government for Appropriation

The 1999 Nigerian Constitution provides for how all revenues accruing to the government should be treated. For this purpose, Section 162 (1) of the Constitution creates the "Federation Account" which is funded by *"All revenues collected by the Government of the Federation, except the proceeds from the personal income tax of the personnel of the armed forces of the Federation, the Nigeria Police Force, the Ministry or department of government charged with responsibility for Foreign Affairs and residents of the Federal Capital Territory, Abuja."*. In addition, Section 80 of the Constitution establishes the "Consolidated Revenue Fund" where *"All revenues or other moneys raised or received by the Federation (not being revenues or other moneys payable under this Constitution or any Act of the National Assembly into any other public fund of the Federation established for a specific purpose) shall be paid into and form one Consolidated Revenue Fund of the Federation."* Section 120 of the Constitution similarly creates a Consolidated Revenue Fund for each State of the Federation so that *"All revenues or other moneys raised or received by a State (not being revenues or moneys payable under this Constitution or any Law of a*

House of Assembly into any other public fund of the State established for a specific purpose shall be paid into and form one Consolidated Revenue Fund of the State." Finally, Section 83 of the Constitution provides that the National Assembly may by law; establish a Contingencies Fund for the Federation. It is in compliance with these provisions of the Constitution that receipts from taxes and levies collected are credited as follows:

Tax Type	Account Credited/Mode of Allocation
Petroleum Profits Tax, Companies Income Tax, Stamp Duties and Capital Gains Tax	Federation Account; and allocated to the three tiers of government on the basis of a sharing formula determined by the Revenue Mobilisation Allocation and Fiscal Commission
Tertiary Education Tax	The Tertiary Education Trust Fund; as required under Section 3 (3) of the Tertiary Education Trust Fund (Establishment) Act 2011. The Board of Trustees of the Fund which is charged with the management of the Fund is required by Section 7 (3) of the Act to distribute the funds among Federal and State tertiary institutions on a ratio of 2:1:1 to universities; polytechnics; and colleges of education respectively

Tax Type	Account Credited/Mode of Allocation
National Information Technology Development Levy	National Information Technology Development Fund; as required under the National Information Technology Development Act 2007
Value Added Tax collected	VAT Pool Account; and shared to all tiers of government in the following ration as prescribed by Section 40 of the Value Added Tax Act: - 50 percent to the States and the Federal Capital Territory; 35 percent to the Local Governments, and - 15 percent to the Federal Government The proviso to Section 40 of the VAT Act (as amended) further provides for the principle of derivation of not less than 20 percent to be reflected in the share of States and Local Governments
Personal Income Tax collected by the FIRS from residents of the FCT	Federal Capital Territory Administration
Personal Income Tax collected by the FIRS from non-residents, members of the Nigerian Police and the Armed Forces, employees of the Federal Ministry of Foreign Affairs	Consolidated Revenue Fund of the Federal Government

Tax Type	Account Credited/Mode of Allocation
Personal Income Tax, levies and charges collected by the State Government as enacted under the Taxes and Levies Act Cap T2 Laws of the Federation of Nigeria 2004	Consolidated Revenue Fund of the State Government

Noteworthy is that even though the FIRSEA 2007 empowers the Service to administer all fees, levies and taxes relating to Oil Exploration License, Oil Mining License, Oil Production License, royalties and rents, this aspect of the Act is yet to be operational and the status quo ante exists.

All payments by taxpayers are made directly into the accounts set up by the Office of the Accountant General of the Federation. Once the tax liability is established, the taxpayer proceeds to any of the Collecting Banks and fills a teller indicating the appropriate tax type and pays into the relevant account. The bank issues the taxpayer with an electronic ticket as evidence of posting and the payment is reflected on the web portal within 24 hours. The Collecting Bank remits all taxes on the same day to one of the Lead Banks via the Interswitch platform for the purpose of reconciliation. The Lead Bank in turn remits all taxes to the Central Bank of Nigeria within two days of receiving same from the Collecting Banks. All electronic tickets issued by the Collecting Banks as well as payments made online are forwarded to the FIRS and cross checked/ reconciled before FIRS receipts of payment are issued to the taxpayer.

The cumulative collection by the Federal Inland Revenue Service for the eight year period between 1996 and 2003 amounted to 2.682 trillion naira. Just four years into the reforms, the collection figure of 2.972 trillion naira for year 2008 alone, was over and above the collection for the preceding eight years put together. The collection figure for 2011 is 4.62 trillion naira. The unprecedented increase in tax revenue for government is attributable to the reforms that have been carried out and are still being carried out to reposition the Nigerian tax system.

CHAPTER FIVE

Recurring Issues and Challenges

Inspite of the various reforms undertaken and still ongoing, the following issues represent issues that still require attention in future modernisation efforts:

a) Compliance Gap
b) Withholding Tax Credit
c) Arrears Build Up and Management
d) Multiple Taxation
e) Use of Consultants in Tax Administration
f) Revenue Allocation

a. Compliance Gap

In terms of overall revenue collection, actual performance has more often than not exceeded set targets. Unfortunately the impressive trend is not always repeated in other financial targets contained in the FIRS Annual Corporate Plans. For example, in 2010, while the overall collection of 2.8 trillion naira exceeded the overall target of 2.5 trillion naira; non oil targets especially of value added tax and personal income tax fell short of the annual targets. Similarly, the 6.76 percent actual ratio of non oil tax to non oil GDP fell short of the targeted 9 percent.

Again in 2011, both VAT and PIT fell short of projections and the ratio of non oil tax to non oil GDP of 6.98 percent was short of the 10 percent target for the year. The figures in the segment on "arrears build-up and management" show that collectively, non-oil taxes are the greatest contributors to arrears build up. The arrangement entered with the Accountant General of the Federation to deduct arrears owed by MDAs from allocations due to them will deter these collection agents from violating the tax laws. Also, the implementation of the presumptive tax and the self assessment provisions in the Personal Income Tax (Amendment) Act 2011 should increase the yield from personal income tax. These and other strategies such as increased taxpayer education and taxpayer segmentation are all geared towards bridging the gap between non oil collection performance against set targets.

b. *Withholding Tax Credit*

While the introduction of Project FACT in 2005 largely addressed the problems of trapped funds and diversion of tax payments; the system did not address the delay in issuing tax receipts and withholding tax credit notes because these were still done manually. In order to automate the crediting of withholding tax, the Service commenced the uploading of withholding tax schedule in 2008. However, technology related problems have made it difficult for the Service to attain the objective of this aspect of the reforms. First, daily printing of the required copies of credit notes is made difficult owing to hardware related problems. Second, software failures lead to the negative reading of withholding tax in the database, duplication of payments and truncation of kobo payments. Third, connectivity problems lead to link failures between headquarters and field offices or service providers. In the light of these challenges, withholding tax credit has been one of the more recurring points of taxpayer dissatisfaction with the Service. It is envisaged that the full implementation of the ITAS Project would address these shortcomings by adopting a software that would credit taxpayers real time thereby dispensing with the need for manual crediting of K cards as it is presently done. As an interim measure, however, the Service is in the process of putting together a Special Task Force to address all outstanding withholding tax issues as a stop gap to the full implementation of ITAS.

c.   *Arrears build up and management*
Tax arrears have become a worrisome phenomenon in the Nigerian tax system. State Governments; MDAs; Local Governments and other categories of agents mandated under the relevant tax laws to withhold tax at source when making payments to third parties either fail to deduct or having deducted, fail to remit to the relevant tax authorities as required by law. Audit and reconciliation

exercises are frequently carried out by FIRS for the purpose of ascertaining the status of liabilities of MDAs, States and Local Governments. However, some of the affected agencies always renege on the payment of the agreed liabilities. The cumulative effect is that billions of Naira of *bona fide* taxes that should have accrued to Government is held back by uncooperative tax collection agents. The most recent exercise in addressing this unwholesome trend involved a meeting between the Accountant General of the Federation and the State counterparts where it was resolved that the liabilities should be reconciled and a reasonable payment plan agreed with each of the State Government with evidence of a sign-off. Failure to meet the agreed payment plan by any State Government would result in the arrears being recovered by deduction at source from their monthly allocation. The summary of total arrears, penalties and interest as at 30th September, 2011 is presented below according to tax type:

i.	Petroleum Profits Tax	N47,041,597,302.51
ii.	Companies' Income Tax/	
	Withholding Tax	N68,731,494,318.81
iii.	Value Added Tax	N58,745,241,842.78
iv.	Education Tax	N11,375,217,512.64
v.	Personal Income Tax/PAYE	N2,558,997,592.46
vi.	Others	N89,928,569.00
vii.	Cumulative Penalties:	N67,376,996,355.90
viii.	Cumulative Interest:	N42,134,093,596.80

Total Arrears   **N298,053,567,090.90**

d. Multiple Taxation

The myriad of taxes and levies imposed on taxpayers in various States across the country constitute a major disincentive to the growth of economies at the State and national levels. In spite of the clear provisions of the Taxes and Levies (Approved List for Collection) Act and the efforts of the Joint Tax Board, incidents of multiple taxation are still commonplace. The problem of multiple taxation arises from:

i. The practice of several agencies of the same government levying and collecting taxes on the same business transaction/activity;

ii. The imposition of taxes by different revenue authorities as goods or services are transported across Local Government or State boundaries; and

iii. Unauthorized persons presuming to collect taxes or levies which in the absence of enabling statutory frameworks amount to extortion

The Joint Tax Board has been at the forefront of the fight against multiple taxation using different media and platforms to raise public consciousness and also galvanize official action against multiple taxation. Some of the steps the Board has encouraged State Governments to take include:

i. Issuance of Executive Orders banning all illegal tax practices.

ii. Constitution of the State Joint Revenue Committee as prescribed by the Personal Income Tax Act to coordinate the activities of revenue collecting agencies at both State and Local Government levels.

iii. Collaboration with relevant law enforcement agencies to ensure proper enforcement of extant laws; for example, sanction all Local Government Councils engaged in illegal tax activities such as the practice of blocking roads to collect taxes.

iv. Publication of the list of authorized taxes as well as avenues the public can take to obtain refund from the State tax authority especially in instances where such taxes had been paid in a different state already. This way the public is duly informed and educated on what taxes are legal and ways to obtain redress in the event of a breach.

These measures will reduce the menace of multiple taxation and make States attractive havens for investment and boost economic activities.

e.   *Use of Consultants in Tax Administration*

The use of consultants in tax administration gained traction during the military era. Proponents of the practice argue that the use of consultants results to higher yields in tax revenue for the government. It must however be pointed out that this argument misses the point which is that the use of consultants in carrying out assessment and collection is illegal. The law permits the use of tax consultants in the provision of services such as training, accounting, management and technical support, all of which improve the capacity of the revenue authorities to deliver on their core mandate of tax collection.

The functions of assessment, collection and accounting for revenues which form the core of tax administration are assigned by law to the Federal Inland Revenue Service at the federal level; State Boards of Internal Revenue at the State level; and Local Government Revenue Committees at the Local Government level. Beyond the issue of legal duty; the power of taxation is an index of sovereignty and the government as the custodian of the sovereign status must not cede it to another party.

Through the efforts of the Joint Tax Board, many States continue to jettison the use of tax consultants and instead invest in human capacity building, technology and other platforms that are necessary to modernize tax administration and enhance the overall capacity of the States' Boards to deliver on their mandates.

f.   Revenue Allocation

The formula for allocating federally collected revenues has always been a topical issue in the country. The Constitution vests all tiers of government with functions and responsibilities; and while also matching these responsibilities with revenue generating powers; a plethora of factors have converged to place undue emphasis on oil revenues as the mainstream of income for government at all levels. Stripped of all verbiage, the sometimes acrimonious debate on revenue allocation between and among different components of the Federation is essentially about drawing sufficient funds to discharge the various responsibilities vested in each tier of government. This explains why the debate on revenue sharing formula usually throws up related subjects such as resource control, derivation and fiscal transfers which are some of the most contentious issues in the practice of fiscal federalism in Nigeria. This trend has seen the proliferation of various factors in the allocation of federally collected revenues to sub-national governments in Nigeria. Presently, Section 162 (2) of the 1999 Constitution enjoins the Revenue Mobilisation, Allocation and Fiscal Commission to advise the President on the appropriate revenue sharing formula while the President upon receipt of the advice, is obliged to table same before the National Assembly. In passing the formula for allocation of revenues from the Federation Account, the National Assembly is enjoined by the same provision of the Constitution to take into consideration the factors of equality of States, population, landmass, terrain, internal revenue generation, population density and derivation; the last not being less than 13 percent of revenue accruing to the Federation Account directly from any natural resources.

The Revenue Allocation Formula Bill which President Obasanjo, on the advice of the Commission, submitted to the National Assembly in December 2002 has not been passed by the National Assembly to date. Before then, the formula used to allocate revenue from the Federation Account was essentially that which was introduced by the Federal Military Government in 1992. Since 2002 however, series of Executive Orders have been used to review the revenue allocation formula. The latest of such Executive Orders was issued in March 2004 and is the basis for allocation of revenue to date. The formula is as follows:

With 13 % Derivation:

Federal Government:	46%
State Government:	23%
Local Government:	18%
Derivation:	13%
Total:	**100%**

Net of 13% Derivation:

Federal Government:	52.68%
State Government:	26.72%
Local Government:	20.60%
Total:	**100%**

The main objectives of the tax system reforms are to widen the economic base and grow non oil revenues. The attainment of these objectives and consequent removal of emphasis on centrally allocated mineral wealth should restore a more agreeable form of fiscal relations among the federating units.

CHAPTER SIX

Global Tax Issues

Global tax issues for immediate and future consideration include:

a)   International partnerships and collaboration
b)   Avoidance of Double Taxation Agreements
c)   Information Exchange
d)   Transfer Pricing
e)   Confidentiality

a.   *International Partnerships and Collaboration*
The Federal Inland Revenue Service is an active player in international associations and organisations including the Commonwealth Association of Tax Administrators, CATA; the African Tax Administrators Forum, ATAF and the Value Added Tax Administrators in Africa, VADA. The Service has not only participated in activities of these organisations outside Nigeria, it has also hosted delegates from other countries at different times in respect of events organised under the auspices of each of these organisations. In the case of ATAF, the Service did not only play a leading role in its formation in 2008, but also continues to play key roles in the development of the

Association. Currently, the Service, along with other countries within the West African sub region are steering the formation of the West African Tax Administrators Forum, WATAF.

All these efforts at international collaboration and partnerships are aimed at sharing experiences to enhance best practices; building capacities to enhance efficiencies and competencies; and addressing problems and challenges of common concern to national revenue authorities.

b.   *Avoidance of Double Taxation Agreements*
An avoidance of double taxation agreement is a reciprocal arrangement between two countries specifying that the income of an individual or profits of a company brought or received into their respective territories should be exempt from tax if the individual or company in question had already paid tax on such income or profits in the other country. The rationale behind these treaties is to encourage international trade and commerce by reducing the cost of doing business internationally. Double taxation agreements (DTAs) usually contain articles specifying the responsibilities and privileges of the contracting States.

Nigeria is signatory to 10 such agreements currently, while negotiations are on-going with several other countries. The countries with which Nigeria operates DTAs currently are the United Kingdom, Pakistan, Belgium, France, The Netherlands, Romania, Canada, South Africa, China and Italy. While others with Denmark, Mauritius, South Korea, Spain and Sweden, are at different stages of domestication. The Service is working on a tax treaty policy and strategy that will determine the priorities of the Service in engaging in such agreements towards improving Nigeria's competitiveness.

The global body that defines the framework for DTAs between developed and developing countries is the Committee of Experts on International Cooperation on Tax Matters. The Committee was established in 1968 as the Ad hoc Group of Experts on Tax Treaties between Developed and Developing Countries and was renamed in 2004. The mandate of the 25 member Committee is to:

i.   Review and update as necessary the *United Nations Model Double Taxation Convention between Developed and Developing Countries* and the *Manual for the Negotiation of Bilateral Tax Treaties between Developed and Developing Countries;*

ii. Provide a framework for dialogue among national tax authorities in order to promote cooperation;

iii. Consider how emerging issues can affect international cooperation in tax matters and develop appropriate recommendations;

iv. Make recommendations for capacity building and technical assistance to developing countries and countries with transitional economies;

v. Give special attention to developing economies and economies in transition with respect to the above issues

Members of the Committee are appointed to a four year term by the Secretary General of the United Nations. The Executive Chairman of the FIRS was appointed to the Committee by the United Nations Secretary General in November 2009. The Executive Chairman heads the Capacity Building Sub-committee. Since 2009, therefore the Service, through the Executive Chairman has been partaking in the meetings of the Committee which are usually held over five days every year in Geneva, and contributing to the actualization of the Committee's mandate.

c.   *Information Exchange*

Information exchange is an essential tool for the development of a sound tax system. There is a need therefore, to develop the tax system in such a way that will permit strong partnership and effective exchange of information among tax authorities within and across national borders. The TIN Project is designed to provide a platform for such interaction between and among Nigeria's federal and sub-national tax authorities. At the international level, Nigeria joined the OECD Global Forum for Transparency and Exchange of Information in 2010 and will be subject to peer review in 2013. The OECD Global Forum on Transparency and Exchange of Information for Tax Purposes provides a multilateral framework within which cooperation in the area of transparency and exchange of information has been carried out by OECD and non-OECD countries since 2000. Through the issuance of the "Model Agreement on Exchange of Information on Tax Purposes" (2002) and the "Enabling Effective Exchange of Information: Availability Standard and Reliability Standard" (2005) the Forum has developed global standards of transparency and exchange of information. In addition, since 2006 the Forum has produced an annual assessment of the legal and administrative framework for transparency and exchange of information in over 80 jurisdictions.

The Forum is working to:

i.   expand its membership and ensure its members participate on equal terms;

ii. agree on how to establish an in-depth peer review process to monitor and review progress made towards full and effective exchange of information; and;

iii. identify mechanisms to speed-up the negotiation and conclusion of agreements to exchange information and to enable developing countries to benefit from the new cooperative initiative in the global tax environment.

Nigeria, through FIRS' membership of organisations such as the Commonwealth Association of Tax Administrators (CATA); African Tax Administrators Forum (ATAF) and Value Added Tax Administrators in Africa (VADA), also engages in information and experience sharing as well as peer review with tax authorities of other countries. The emphasis is to build capacities; promote global best practices and tackle issues that commonly affect tax authorities in all jurisdictions. Furthermore, avoidance of double taxation agreements usually contain a clause obligating the competent authorities of the contracting States to exchange such information as may be necessary to give effect to the objectives of the agreement.

The conclusion of the ITAS and TIN Projects are designed to provide a platform for such interaction between the Service and its stakeholders including international tax bodies and national tax authorities.

d. *Transfer Pricing*

Transfer pricing encompasses the setting, analysis, documentation and adjustment of charges among related parties for goods, services, or use of property. It relates to the system of setting prices for the transfer of goods, services and intangibles between or among parties under the same group operating in more than one tax jurisdiction. Transfer pricing is a major concern not only for tax authorities, but also for multinational enterprises operating in more than one tax jurisdiction.

Tax legislations and regulations differ from one tax jurisdiction to another and there is the need for multinational business entities to comply with all these requirements. Tax administrators in these jurisdictions have a duty to impose taxes on these multinationals, but must do so in a fair manner. Fairness can be achieved only when each tax administrator correctly determines the income and expenses of the multinational enterprise attributable to its own jurisdiction. The Service is interested in transfer pricing because plugging the avenues for tax fraud and avoidance in intra-group transactions represent a potential for high revenue yield. The interest of the Service lies in ensuring that the transfer prices for intra-group transactions within its jurisdiction reflect the open market situation so as to ensure that revenue accruable to Government is not compromised.

Between December 2010 and June 2011, the Service in partnership with the OECD and the ATAF organised series of capacity building workshops on transfer pricing issues within and outside the country for employees of the Service. As follow up on these trainings, the

Modernisation Department of the Service is working on modalities to build further capacity within the Service on issues of transfer pricing. Also, the Tax Policy Department has produced a draft manual on transfer pricing guidelines and the document is awaiting the approval of Management in order to become operational.

e.   *Confidentiality*

The confidentiality of information obtained from taxpayers, tax authorities (local and international) and other sources must be maintained. This is one of the arguments against the use of tax consultants and tax contractors. Involving them in the core functions of tax administration will not only compromise the confidentiality of information sources but also confer on the consultants undue advantage as information obtained by them in the course of tax administration could be converted to personal benefit.

*9 7 8 9 7 8 4 8 7 7 6 8 8 *